Freedom
Is Blogging
in Your
Underwear

FREEDOM
IS BLOGGING
IN YOUR
UNDERWEAR

Hugh
MacLeod

PORTFOLIO / PENGUIN

PORTFOLIO / PENGUIN
Published by the Penguin Group
Penguin Group (USA) Inc., 375 Hudson Street, New York, New York 10014, U.S.A. •
Penguin Group (Canada), 90 Eglinton Avenue East, Suite 700, Toronto, Ontario,
Canada M4P 2Y3 (a division of Pearson Penguin Canada Inc.) • Penguin Books Ltd,
80 Strand, London WC2R 0RL, England • Penguin Ireland, 25 St. Stephen's Green,
Dublin 2, Ireland (a division of Penguin Books Ltd) • Penguin Books Australia Ltd, 250
Camberwell Road, Camberwell, Victoria 3124, Australia (a division of Pearson
Australia Group Pty Ltd) • Penguin Books India Pvt Ltd, 11 Community Centre, Pan-
chsheel Park, New Delhi – 110 017, India • Penguin Group (NZ), 67 Apollo Drive,
Rosedale, Auckland 0632, New Zealand (a division of Pearson New Zealand Ltd) •
Penguin Books (South Africa) (Pty) Ltd, 24 Sturdee Avenue, Rosebank, Johannes-
burg 2196, South Africa

Penguin Books Ltd, Registered Offices:
80 Strand, London WC2R 0RL, England

First published in 2012 by Portfolio / Penguin,
a member of Penguin Group (USA) Inc.

10   9   8   7   6   5   4   3   2   1

Some of the selections in this book appeared on the author's Web site,
gapingvoid.com.

LIBRARY OF CONGRESS CATALOGING IN PUBLICATION DATA
MacLeod, Hugh, 1965–
Freedom is blogging in your underwear / Hugh MacLeod.
p.   cm.
ISBN 978-1-59184-485-3
1. Internet—Humor.   2. Creative ability—Humor.   I. Title.
PN6231.I62M33 2012
818'.602—dc23   2012000408

Printed in the United States of America
Set in Akzidenz-Grotesk Pro
Designed by Daniel Lagin

Contents

CONTENTS

Freedom Is Blogging in Your Underwear

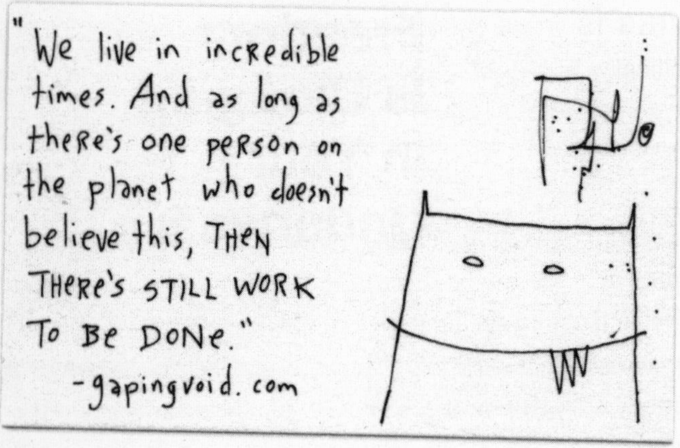
"We live in incredible times. And as long as there's one person on the planet who doesn't believe this, THEN THERE'S STILL WORK TO BE DONE."
-gapingvoid.com

Introduction:
It's All About Freedom

THIS IS A BOOK ABOUT FREEDOM. MORE SPE-
cifically, it's a book about the personal freedom that the
Internet allows all of us to have, to greater or lesser degrees:
the personal freedom I discovered from the wonderful world
of blogging; the freedom I hope everybody will eventually
discover for themselves; the freedom, I believe, that will per-
manently and irrevocably change the world for the better. At
the time of this writing, my blog, gapingvoid.com, turned ten
years old. Having a blog, a voice, having my own media,
utterly changed my life. Suddenly my career as a cartoonist
wasn't dependent on other people: the "gatekeepers"—
publishers, editors, Hollywood executives, etc., etc. Suddenly I had direct contact with my audience. They had direct
contact with me. I could just do my thing, without having to
wait for somebody else to give me the "green light," somebody else to write a check. I didn't have to wait around for
somebody else to deem me "worthy." . . . This gave me the
freedom I spent most of my adult life searching for, the same
freedom I believe we're ALL searching for, in one way or
another.

Careerwise, blogging gave me everything. Even in the early days, the benefits of blogging were so glaringly obvious to me that I couldn't understand why more people weren't doing it. Ten years later, I still can't. So I decided to write a book about it; maybe I could help other people find this freedom, too. Like I said, I'm a cartoonist. I don't consider myself a "blogging professional." I don't consider myself a "social media authority." That being said, I believe my experience as one of the very early visual artists to totally establish their careers via this wonderful new medium might help folks understand not only how powerful blogging is, but WHY it's powerful and WHY it matters. And once you can understand this, I believe, your life will be quickly transformed, same as mine was. . . . Included in the book are some of my trademark "cartoons drawn on the back of business cards," which I was drawing on the side while putting this book together. Some are here to amuse. Some are here to mix things up. Some are here to inspire you and make you think. And some do it all.

This book is dedicated to Alex Korman (the son of my business partner, Jason). He's a wonderful young man who is quickly and joyfully learning that the best way to be successful, in this hypercompetitive world of ours, is to find something you REALLY love doing and then kick ass at it. And blogging is one of the best ways I know of to find that out. Exactly.

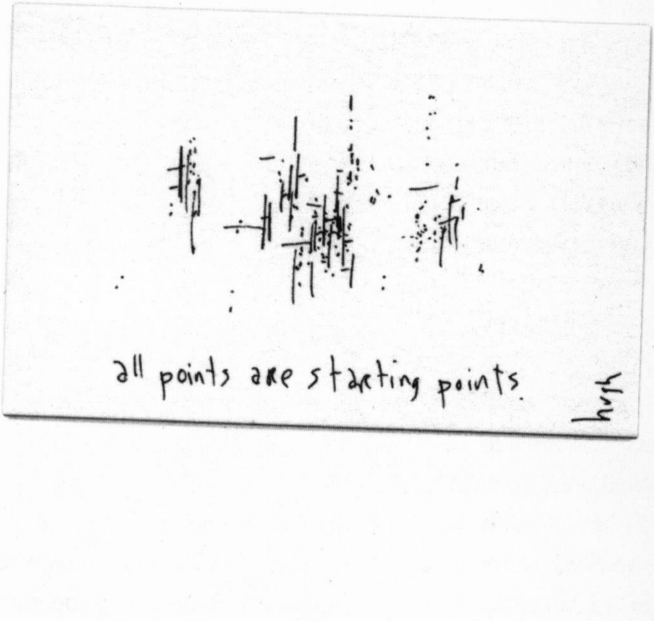
all points are starting points.
hugh

don't tell
me how to live.

tell me
how
i'm alive.

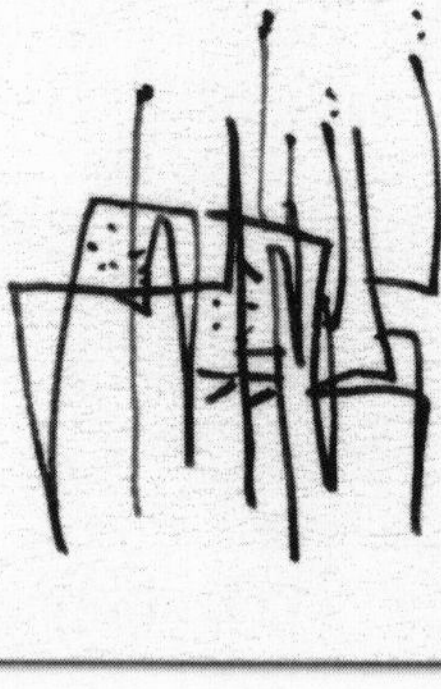

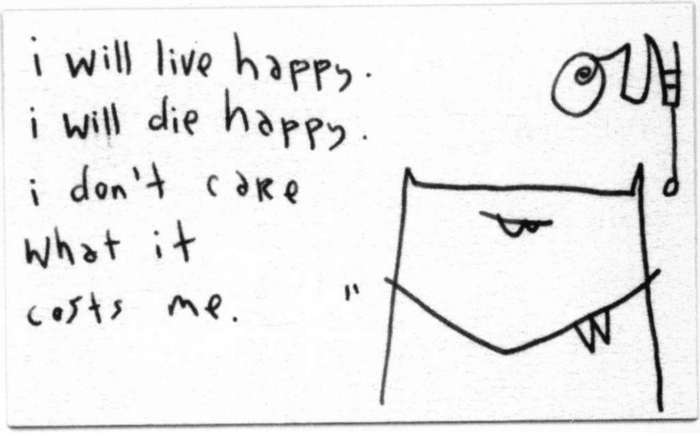
i will live happy.
i will die happy.
i don't care
what it
costs me. "

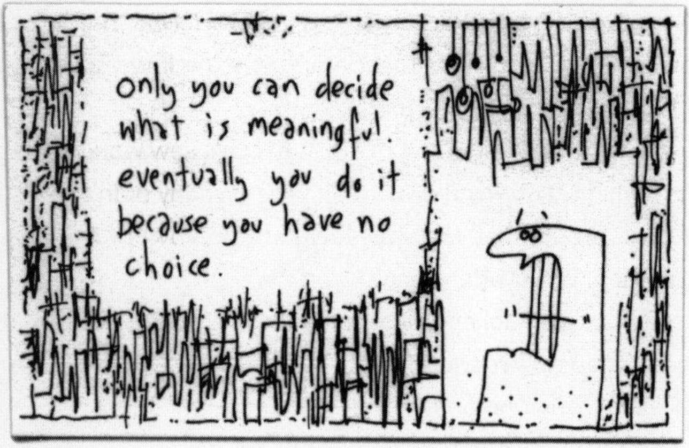
only you can decide
what is meaningful.
eventually you do it
because you have no
choice.

A few years ago, I was watching Henry Rollins, the famed punk rocker and performance artist, being interviewed on TV by some clever wee media twinkie.

Twinkie was criticizing Rollins about his new work, saying something like, why did you do it this way, why didn't you do it your old, normal way, will your fans approve of this new direction, yada yada yada. . . .

Rollins just looked at Twinkie and said, "I thought rock 'n' roll was about Freedom . . . ?"

Twinkie had no answer.

Henry was right. It's about Freedom.

And that's what the Internet is also REALLY about, isn't it?

Finding your freedom. Finding your wings.

Using a computer instead of a guitar.

This is the appeal of the Internet—the sense of freedom that it gives us, the kind of people it allows us to be. The fact that it happens via computers is secondary.

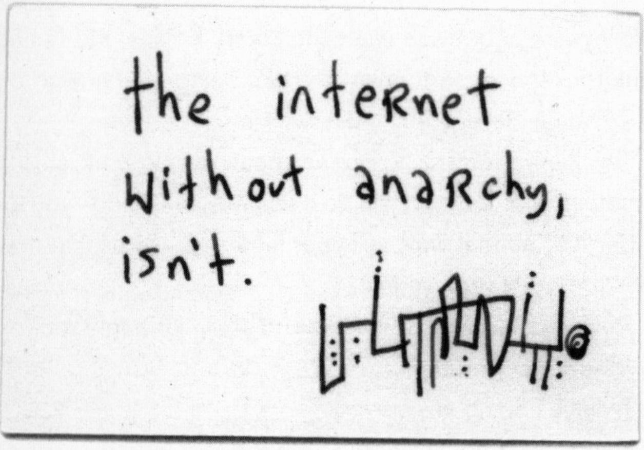
the internet
without anarchy,
isn't.

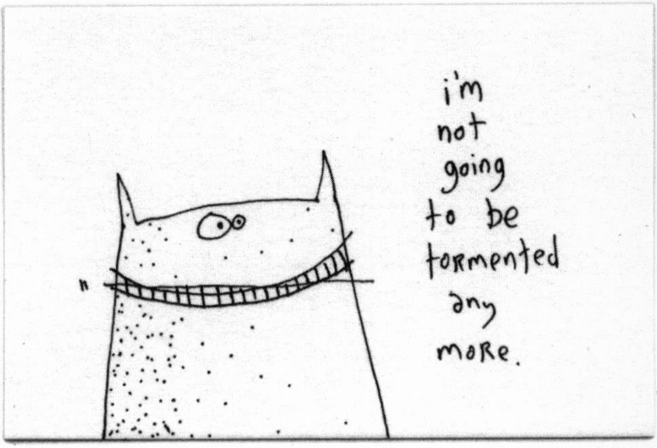
i'm
not
going
to be
tormented
any
more.

i got
an apartment
and a job
and a
girlfriend
and a
gym
member-
ship
i am a higher being

the good news is:
you're not going to die.
the bad news is:
you're not going to live.

Blogging Gave Me Wings

Through blogging, my cartoons have reached millions of people.

Through my blog, my entire career as a cartoonist, author, and marketing guy was made.

I met my girlfriend through my blog.

I met my business partner through my blog.

I meet all my clients and customers through my blog. They all start off as readers.

My blog gave me everything.

My blog gave me my freedom.

Freedom to get stuff done more easily.

Freedom to connect with other like-minded people, regardless of where I live.

Freedom to do what I want. Freedom from the stuff I don't.

That same Freedom our forefathers fought and died for. That same fight for Freedom that got our boys killed back on Normandy's beaches.

The Freedom to express ourselves.

The Freedom to be ourselves.

The Freedom to be who we were born to be—the artist within us all.

The Freedom to blog in our underwear, if we want.

It has arrived. It is here.

Life will never be the same. And thank goodness for that.

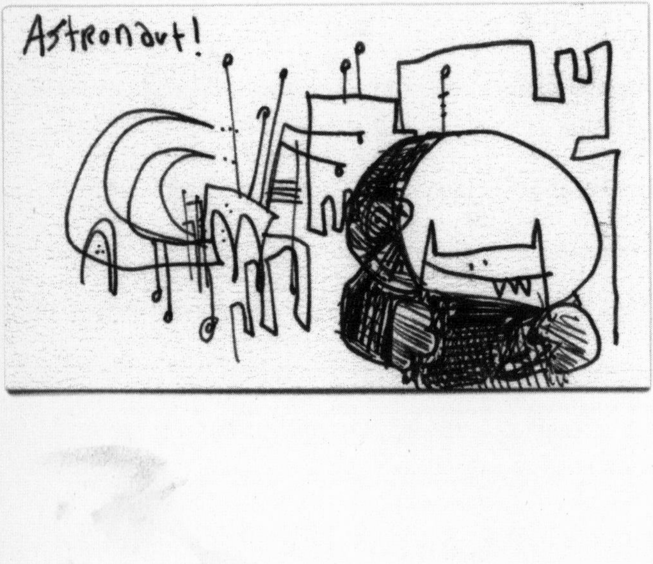
Astronaut!

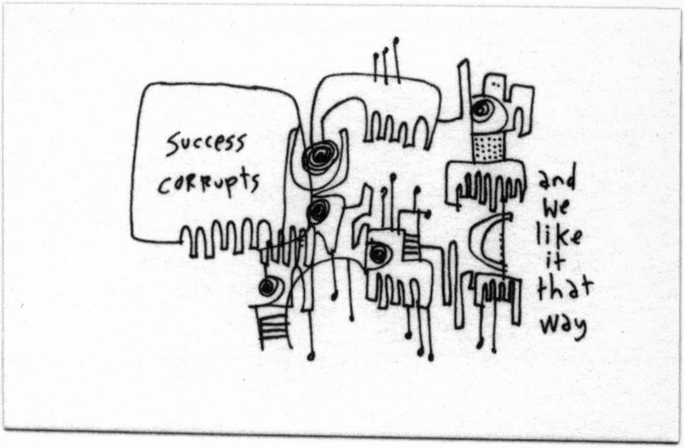
success corrupts
and we like it that way

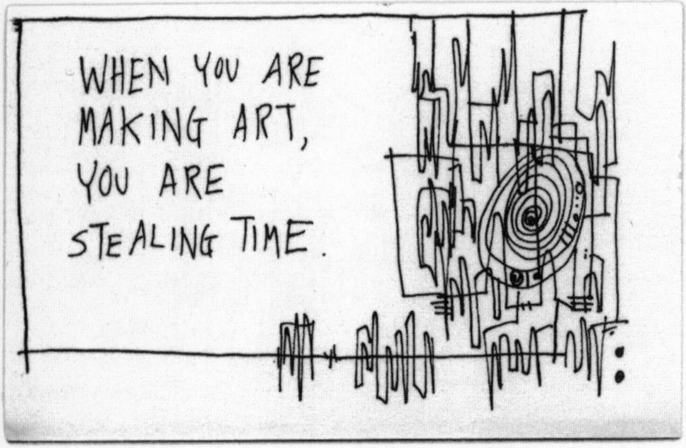
WHEN YOU ARE
MAKING ART,
YOU ARE
STEALING TIME.

a generation ago,
an artist needed
new york.

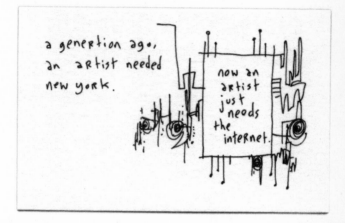

now an
artist
just
needs
the
internet.

The Internet Is Revolution. Profound Revolution.

SOME PEOPLE CLAIM THE INTERNET'S EFFECT is as profound as any major revolution that has preceded it: the Industrial, the French, the American, Russian, Chinese, or what have you.

They are right to do so.

And better yet, so far it hasn't required the usual horrors of revolution: barricades being stormed, monarchs being decapitated, peasants starving by the millions. Instead we have a lot of mommy bloggers uploading photos of their cats and tech geeks ranting on about some inferior product. Or whatever.

entrepreneurship
can't be
taught.

but it can
be
unleashed....

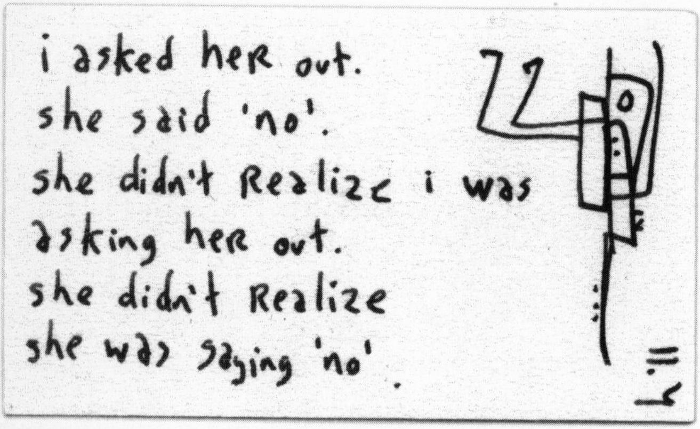
i asked her out.
she said 'no'.
she didn't realize i was
asking her out.
she didn't realize
she was saying 'no'.

i'm going to reach
enlightenment WAY
sooner than all those
OTHER assholes......

human
mess.
human
chaos...

The Internet Is a Miracle

EVEN PEOPLE (INCLUDING ME) WHO ARE OLD enough to remember life before the Internet have a hard time remembering what life was like before it. Everything you need to know and everybody you need to talk to are right there, a simple click away. No traveling thousands of miles to talk to somebody. No schlepping down to the library just to find something out. No not knowing where the good Chinese restaurants in town are. No having to get on the freeway in order to go buy something.

It's a miracle. One that we already have learned to take for granted.

~~Silicon Valley~~
everwhere

power is to be pitied,
not envied.

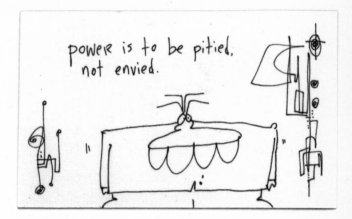

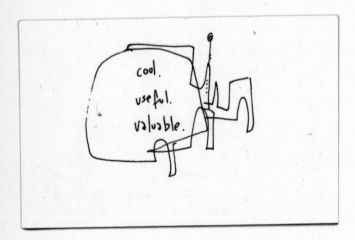

cool.

useful.

valuable.

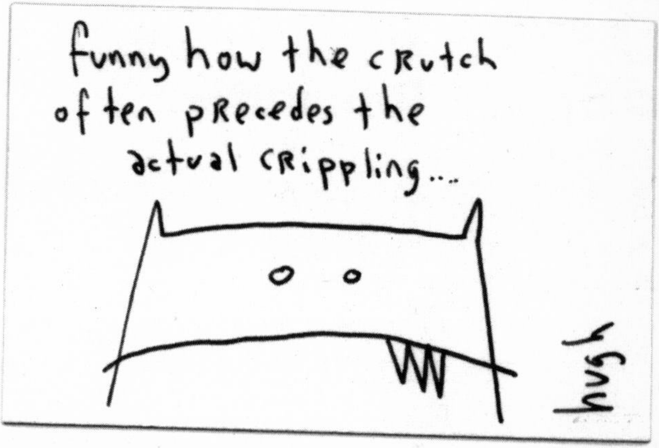
funny how the crutch often precedes the actual crippling...
hugh

It's Never Been Easier to Spot a Bullshitter

IT'S NEVER BEEN EASIER TO FIND OUT WHETHER what someone's told you is true or not. Just go online and find out what everyone else is saying about it. Just go online and find out what they're saying about that person who told you so. You'll find out soon enough whether or not your source is a bullshitter.

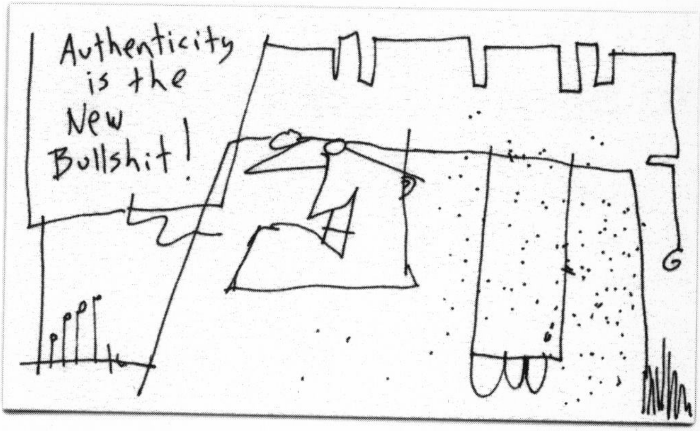
Authenticity is the New Bullshit!

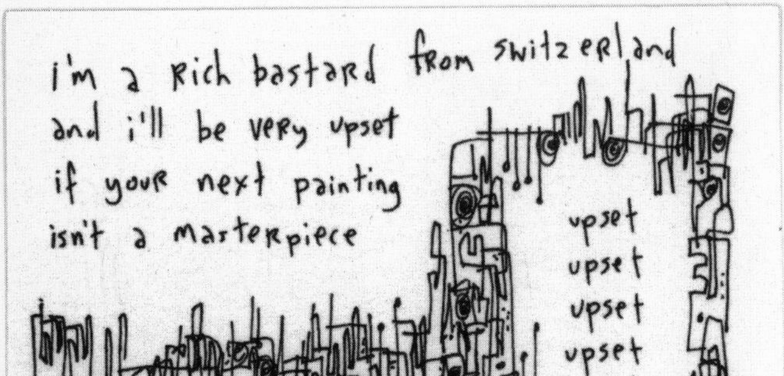
i'm a rich bastard from switzerland
and i'll be very upset
if your next painting
isn't a masterpiece
upset
upset
upset
upset
upset

don't get old
don't get sick
don't get evicted
don't get fired
don't leave new york.

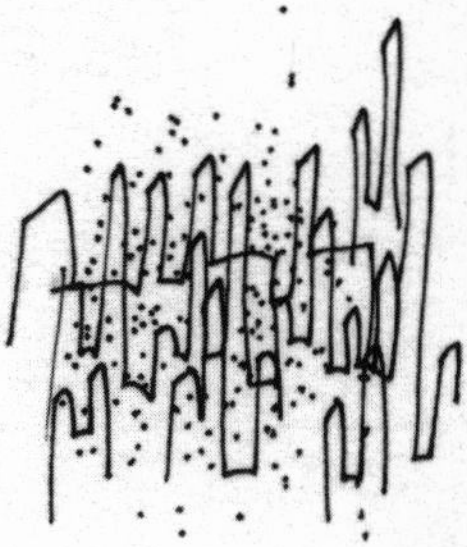

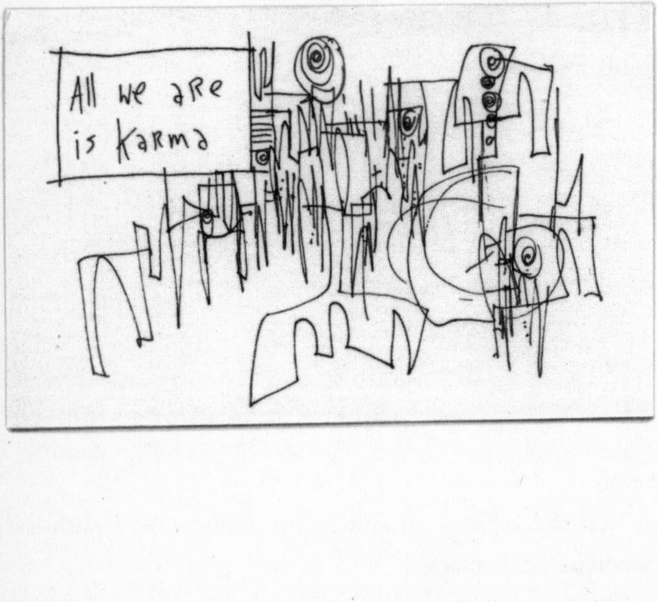
All we are
is Karma

The Internet Keeps Us Honest

IF WE SCREW SOMEBODY OVER, IT'S SAFE TO assume it'll be on the Internet within nanoseconds. "Hugh promised this but only delivered that." "Hugh said this, but actually this is what happened."

When you've been on the Internet long enough, you just assume that whatever you did, good or bad, will appear somewhere. So you suddenly start caring whether what you said was the truth or not. If what you did was honest or not. If who you are is good or not.

The Internet makes us behave ourselves. The Internet makes us accountable.

The Internet keeps it real.

The Internet is Karma.

i like
being
alive

i just wish i was
better at it.

vanity

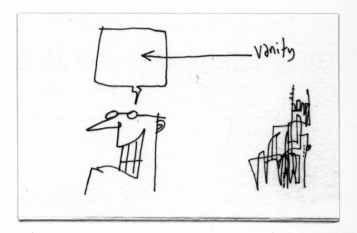

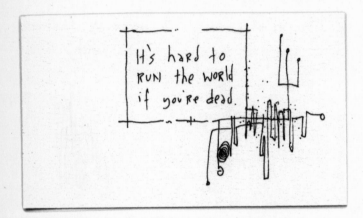

It's hard to
RUN the WORLD
if you're dead.

hate
me
i
need
the
money.

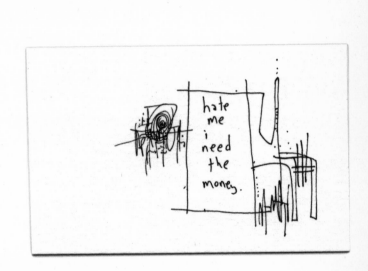

"Crofting" Is the New World of Work

MY GRANDFATHER WAS A SCOTTISH HIGHLANDS "crofter"—i.e., a small-time, mostly self-sufficient tenant farmer with his own little patch of land, who raised sheep and grew potatoes, turnips, and other stuff. And as I wrote in my second book, *Evil Plans*: hey, guess what—we're all crofters now. Even people with secure day jobs in big corporations. Thanks to the Internet, we all have a little electronic "croft"—an electronic smallholding—to call our own: what is commonly referred to as our own digital identity, which we can cultivate, like a small farm, however we see fit.

The good news is that, unlike my grandfather, we don't have to spend our whole lives growing potatoes and shearing sheep for a mere pittance. We can sell things people find valuable—art and cartoons in my case, maybe consulting gigs or whatever in your case. . . .

The Internet makes all this possible.

We all hang out
at starbucks
with our
laptops open
yeah baby you
know you want
it yeah
baby

all
art
is
economics

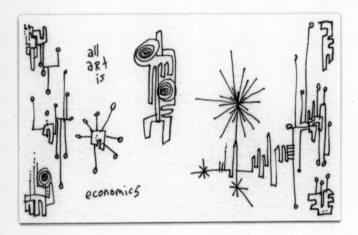

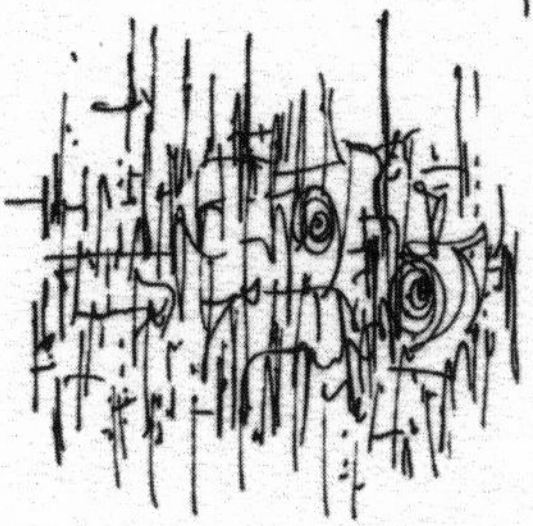

this fine life i have
is paid for by
kissing a lot of
tasty, sweet
ass....

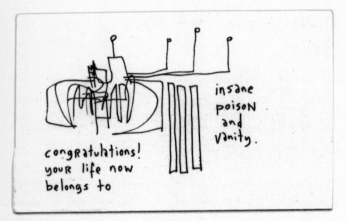

insane
poison
and
vanity.

congratulations!
your life now
belongs to

Forget the Latest Shiny Object

ONE THING THAT IS TRUE ABOUT THE INTERNET is that new stuff always comes along: Google, Facebook, Twitter, Instagram, cat blogs, geek blogs, mommy blogs, tech blogs, lawyer blogs, art blogs, and whatever else might be the flavor of the month.

And like all mortals, we confuse the latest shiny object with Reality. So suddenly we find ourselves losing sleep because we don't have enough Google juice or Twitter followers or Facebook friends, or some Internet celebrity hasn't linked to us.

When actually, all the Internet is, as Doc Searls said, is a bunch of protocols that "allow us to get along." Protocols allow us to talk to each other. The stuff in the middle, the stuff that separates us, the stuff that directly makes use of these protocols—hosting companies, Web sites, blogging platforms, microblogging platforms, etc.—matter far less.

You're on one end of the wire. Just think about who's on

the other end of the wire, and what you can do for them. Worry less about the wire. Worry less about the shiny objects in the middle.

Just worry about MAKING your own stuff, and the rest of the Internet will look after itself.

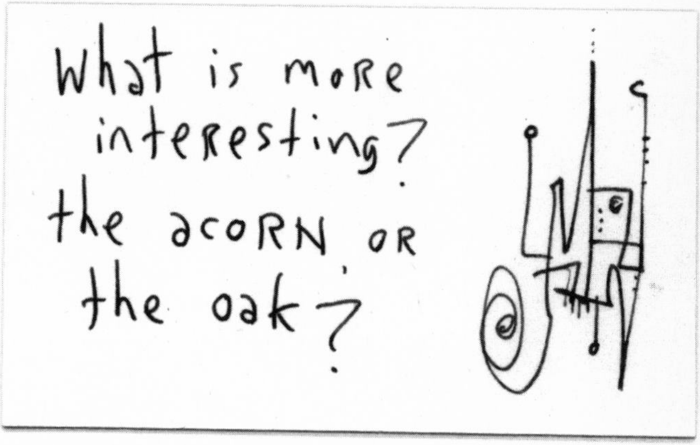
what is more interesting?
the acorn or the oak?

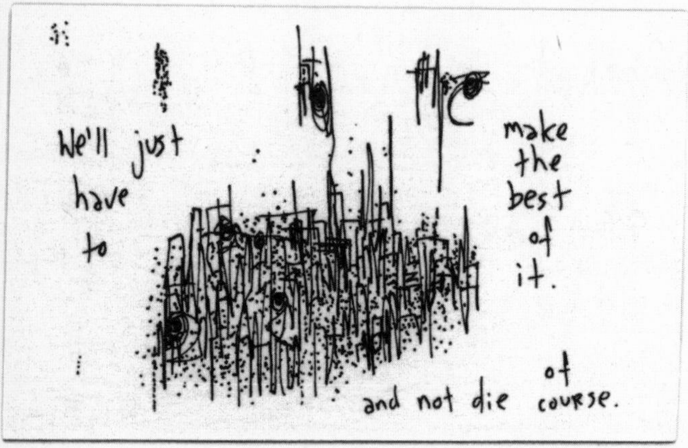
We'll just have to
make the best of it.
and not die of course.

A CRAZY LIFE OF ENDLESS MUNDANE EVENTS

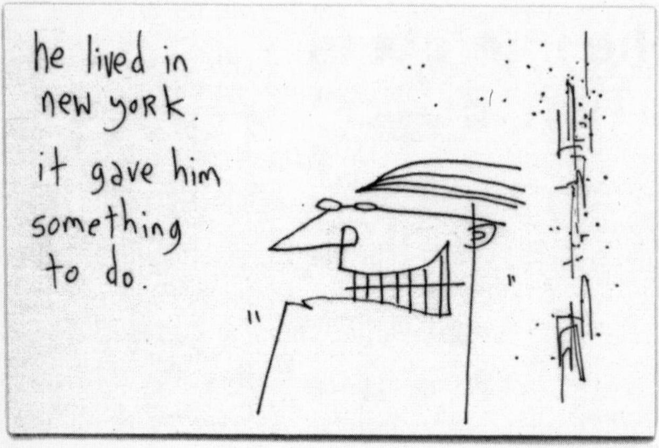
he lived in
new york.
it gave him
something
to do.

The Internet Is a Time Suck

IF YOU'RE LIKE ME, YOU SPEND FAR TOO MUCH time on the Internet. But hey, that's how I make my living, so at least I have an excuse. . . .

It's easy to surf the Internet, the same way it's easy to surf late-night TV. And it too can make you fat, slothful, dissatisfied, and depressed for the exact same reason.

When you're talking to people on the Internet, are you really talking to them? Or is the "conversation" just an excuse to not make meaningful contact? To not get something truly interesting done?

Just because there's interaction going on doesn't mean there's any interaction going on.

Think about it.

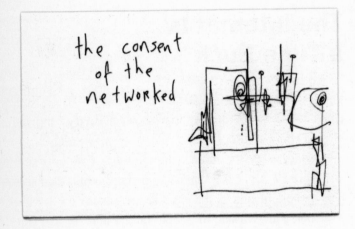

the consent
of the
networked

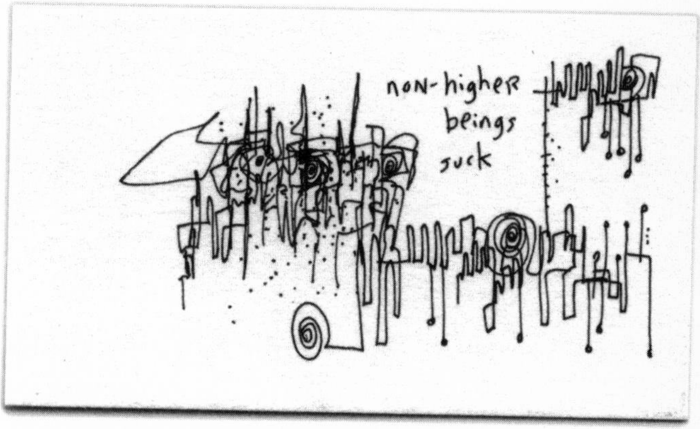
non-higher
beings
suck

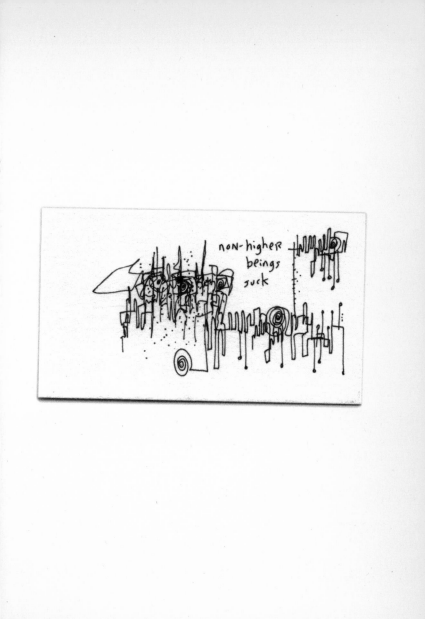

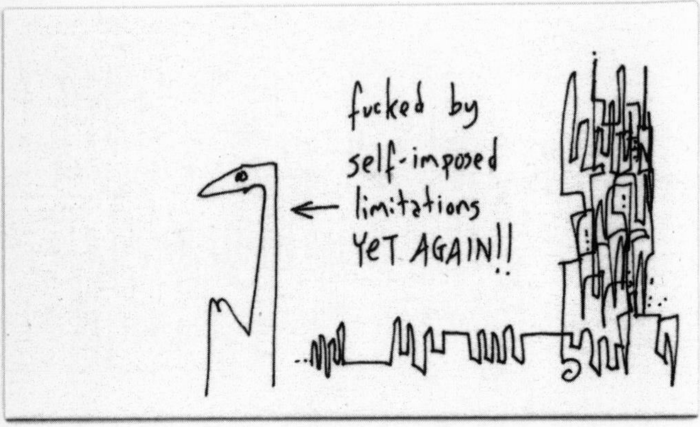
fucked by
self-imposed
limitations
YET AGAIN!!

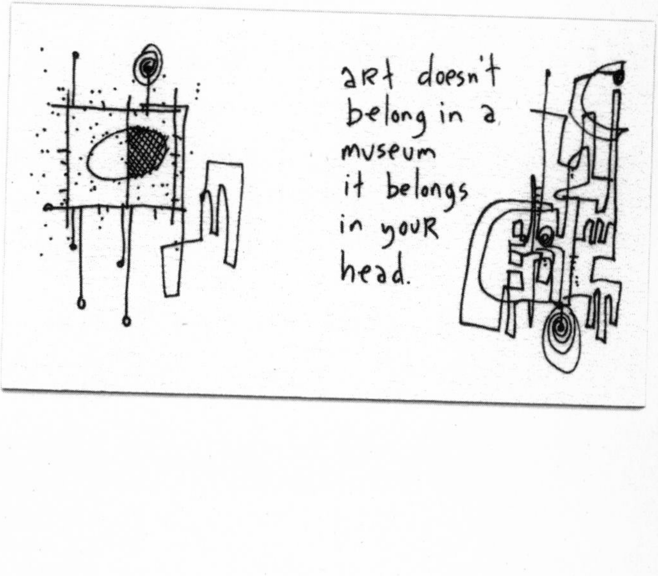
art doesn't
belong in a
museum
it belongs
in your
head.

Bring New Light to What Life Might Be

MOST PEOPLE WHO READ MY BLOG ARE CRE-ative people. That's not just an opinion—that's just how it is. And I enjoy conversing with these very creative people, not just because they are my "fans" but because they *bring new light to what life might be.*

Bring new light to what life might be: that's what Creativity means. That's why you were born; that's why you are here: to bring some new "light," some new angle, to the human condition—if not to the broader world in general, then at least to your family and the people around you.

Not everybody believes this. Not everybody acts on this. That's fine; it's their life, their choice.

However, if you DO have that capacity within yourself and you DON'T act upon it, then everything around you turns to desert.

That's why I like talking to people who read my blog. We're all trying to find a way to find the new light. We're all trying to find out where the new life might be.

karma lasts forever.
karma is eternal.

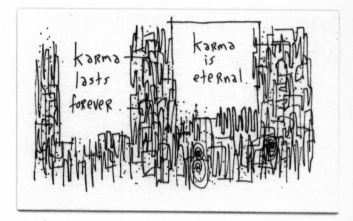

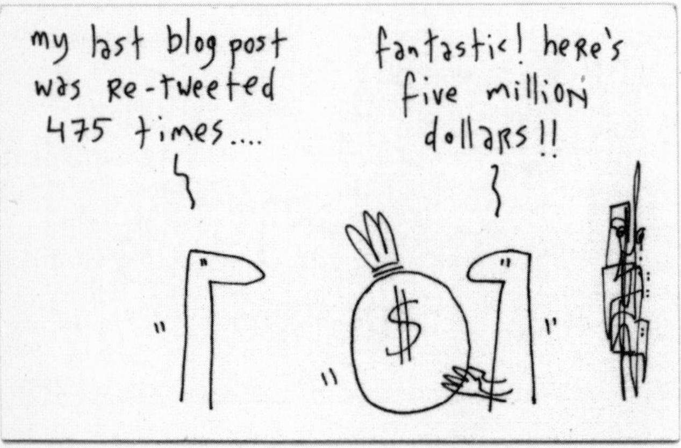
my last blog post was re-tweeted 475 times....
fantastic! here's five million dollars!!

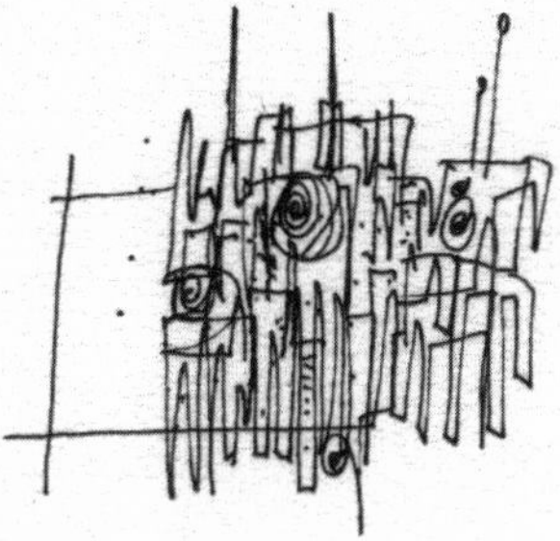

You're only been dead five minutes and already they're beginning to forget about you....

fleeting
moments
beauty
one
day
no more.

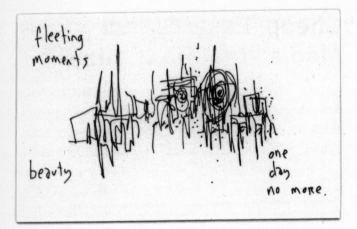

"Cheap, Easy, Global Media" Is Here to Stay

AS ANYONE WHO READS TECHCRUNCH WILL know, the "Is Blogging Dead?" riff likes to rear its ugly head on the Web again and again. One or twice a year, at least.

Well, before we all get dressed up in our best funeral gear, let me say it one more time: **The big story is not about blogging.** It's not about Twitter, YouTube, Facebook, Posterous, or whatever. And it certainly is not about Internet rock stars like Mike Arrington, Tim O'Reilly, Tim Ferriss, or whatever so-called "A-lister" you care you mention.

As I said in my 2010 book *Evil Plans*, it's all about what Clay Shirky said way back in 2004, in a wonderful interview he did for *Gothamist*:

> So forget about blogs and bloggers and blogging and focus on this—the cost and difficulty of publishing absolutely anything, by anyone, into a global medium, just got a whole lot lower. And the effects of that

increased pool of potential producers is going to be vast.

I had coffee with Clay in San Francisco a wee while ago. A totally great guy. We didn't talk about blogs much. Nor did we talk much about Twitter or Facebook or whatever.

We talked about something conceptually far simpler: **Cheap. Easy. Global. Media.**

CheapEasyGlobal is the big story. And it's here now. It has arrived. And it's permanent. And there's not a damn thing anyone can do about it, save for a nuclear holocaust.

And yes, the changes will be vast. In fact, they already are.

in nature,
when bad
things happen,
it's usually
far more
permanent
than when
good things happen.

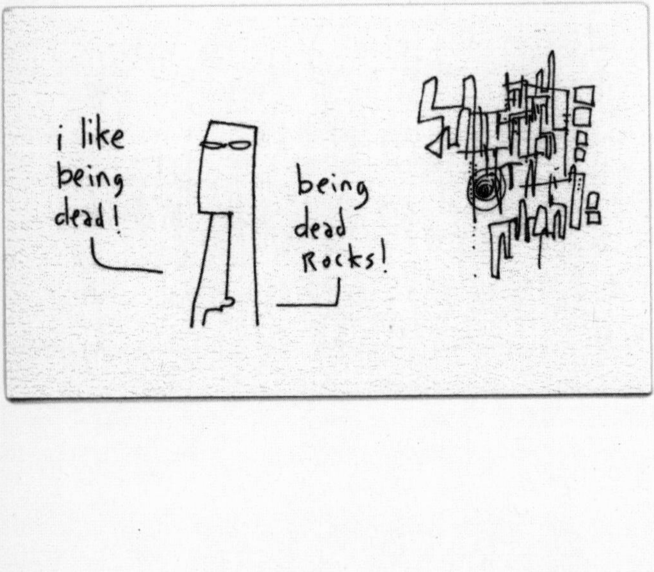

i like being dead!
being dead Rocks!

Stress is the price you pay

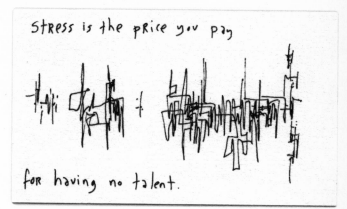

for having no talent.

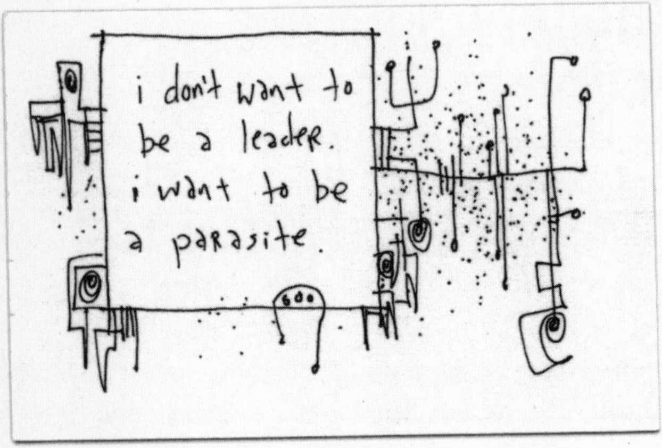
i don't want to
be a leader.
i want to be
a parasite.

The Internet Eats the "Ignorance Premium" for Breakfast

PEOPLE HAVE BEEN PESSIMISTIC ABOUT THE future, about the economy, for a while now.

That's because the world has changed.

The world hasn't changed because some Wall Street bankers screwed up. The world hasn't changed because some politician lied on TV. They've always done that. They always screw up or lie or both. Whatever.

This time, the world has changed because the Internet changed it.

Back in the nineteenth century, the British were able to maintain their empire not because they were cute and nice and fun and cuddly, nor because they were vicious, greedy, genocidal psychopaths. The real reason, basically, was that they knew more than the OTHER guy.

And they didn't know more because they had biologically bigger brains or stronger bodies than everybody else. They knew more because they got lucky. They had the historical good fortune to be at the right place at the right time—to have discovered property rights, freedom of speech, capitalism, collaborative science, entrepreneurship, religious tolerance, equality before the law, and all that other good stuff we Westerners now take for granted.

But eventually, after a century or so, the gap between what the Brits knew and what everybody else knew started to evaporate. Other people started catching up—the Germans, the Americans, the French, the Russians, and the Japanese; the list goes on.

Taking the British Empire down with it.

And what happened to the Brits then is now happening to everybody else, only much quicker. This isn't happening over decades; it's happening within days.

The Internet makes it harder for us to know more than the other guy.

The Internet makes it FAR easier for people to know that the deal we're offering them isn't really such a good deal. That there are thousands of other better deals out there, just a mouse click away.

This is true whether you're a mom 'n' pop joint, a large corporation, or, yes, a nation-state.

The Internet erodes the "Ignorance Premium."

Economists call this "Asymmetrical Information." I call it the Ignorance Premium. It's how most people make a living.

The reason you pay a heart surgeon the big bucks is because he knows A LOT more about saving your life than you do. You pay a plumber or a lawyer or a carpenter an arm and a leg for the same reason.

They all know more than you do.

And it's not just the highly skilled tradesmen and professionals. Restaurants know more than you about how to cook exotic food. Singles bars know more than you about how to attract large clusters of the opposite sex.

Because knowledge is now so much easier to share with the Internet, you're in trouble if the only reason you can make a living is because somebody is too lazy to easily find out what you know with just a quick click of a mouse.

The Internet eats the Ignorance Premium for breakfast.

Vapid,
ludicRous
people
wandeRing
why
nobody
caRes.

All lives end in Failure. The question is whether one Fails with Honor.

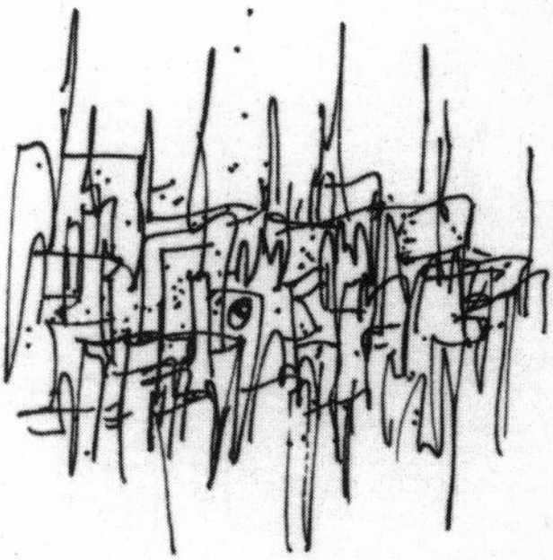

i have bad news for people who don't believe in the afterlife.
too late. you're already living it.

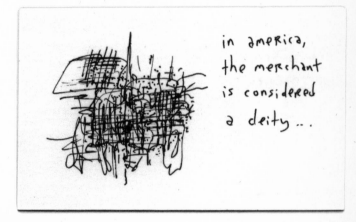

in america,
the merchant
is considered
a deity...

The Internet Makes the Easy Stuff Easier. Unfortunately, the Hard Stuff Is Still Just as Hard.

I'M A FULL-TIME CARTOONIST. I BASICALLY MAKE art for a living.

And I use the Internet to sell it. I don't do galleries or get my stuff in newspapers. I just publish it on my blog, I post it in my online gallery, I send it along in my daily newsletter, and then people buy it.

Yes, it's easy. Compared to getting discovered by the *New York Times*, United Features Syndicate, or a blue-chip New York art gallery, it's REALLY easy.

But no matter how easy it gets, art still remains an expensive, time-consuming, labor-intensive, pain-in-the-ass thing to make.

I still get up early in the morning and get to work, every day. I still do the long hours, every day.

And whatever it is that you do, the hard stuff—the REALLY hard stuff that people actually value—will be no different.

The Internet is just something that allows us to connect easily—it can't lead our lives for us while we just sit around in our underwear. . . .

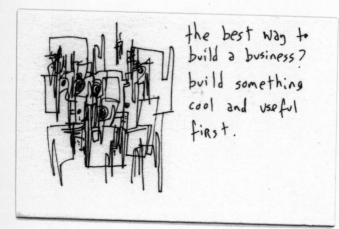

the best way to
build a business?
build something
cool and useful
first.

karma happens.

SINK
HOLE
OF
BAD
KARMA !!

HATE is just
a WORD FOR
somebody you
LOVE but no
longer believe
in.

The Internet Allows Us to Be Small, Quirky, Unique, Ferociously Independent, and Still Able to Survive

I WAS THINKING RECENTLY ABOUT THEY MIGHT Be Giants, an indie band I've been following off and on for over twenty years.

TMBG have been together for nearly thirty years.

TMBG never really had major mainstream success. They've just done their quirky little thing from their happy little corner of Brooklyn.

The Internet stuff that most musical acts now use to promote their work—e-mail newletters, MySpace, Facebook, Twitter, etc., etc.—they were doing it first, pretty much before anybody else. That's what makes them interesting. They were pioneers. They had to be, if the band was to survive.

To be small, quirky, unique, ferociously independent, and still able to survive.

They are a true "global microbrand." Their example has always been huge inspiration to me.

Thanks to the Internet, we FINALLY live in a world where folks like TMBG can exist. Thanks to the Internet, TMBG's business model is easier to maintain and more accessible to more people than at any time in history. A much-needed antidote to the shopping mall, to the tedious, insatiable maw that is mainstream, celebrity-driven culture.

This is huge. This is permanent. And people are only JUST beginning to realize this.

believe
in me.

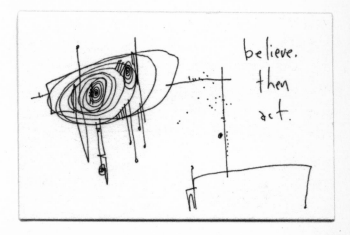

believe.
then
act.

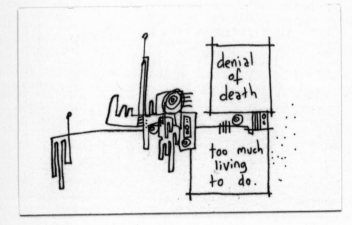

denial
of
death

too much
living
to do.

where there's kindness
there is
hope.

The Internet Allows
Small Magic to Happen

THE CORNER BISTRO WAS MY REGULAR WATER-
ing hole back when I lived in the West Village in the late
1990s, back when I was first drawing my trademark "cartoons on the back of business cards."

I'd stumble in there late at night a few times a week. Great
hamburgers.

Jeff would pour me a drink. Maker's Mark on the rocks.

Jeff was a photographer. Nice guy. Great bartender. He
liked my cartoons. I'd show him the new ones. He'd tell me
which ones he liked.

I liked Jeff. We had a rapport. This was before I was ever
published. This was long before blogging or Web 2.0.

This was when I was still unknown. A nobody. A goofball
nobody in a tweed jacket, who would sit at the end of the
bar for hours on end, doodling on the back of business
cards for no reason.

So when I was in New York last February, I walked into the Corner Bistro, again.

Jeff was working; he's still there. He's married and has a kid now. He's got a regular day job doing something else, but tends bar once a week for the hell of it.

He remembered me!

I give him a signed copy of my book *Ignore Everybody* (I had brought one with me, with the express intention of giving it to him), the book that was inspired by my days when I lived in New York—my lazy weekends in the West Village, my Saturday afternoons at the Corner Bistro, enjoying a drink, watching the cabs through the window driving up Hudson, as Charlie Parker played on the best jukebox in Manhattan.

It was really good to see Jeff again. It had been over a decade. It felt like coming home. It was nice to be able to say to somebody from the old 'hood, "Yeah. I made it. Finally."

"This is an awesome New York story," he said.

He's right. It is.

And without the Internet, of course, none of this would've have happened.

People like to think that Offline and Online are different places, that what happens in Cyberspace bears no relation to Meatspace.

Trying to see them as separate is a mistake. It will just cause you pain.

The Internet is not some add-on to your life; the Internet is central to your life.

Now don't get scared. You can still go outside and roll in the grass. Real life still exists. Just as life on the Internet does.

FREE
SPEECH
ISN'T

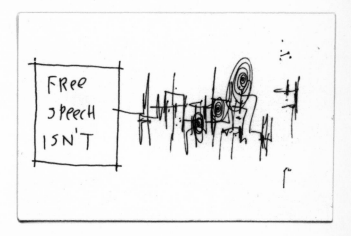

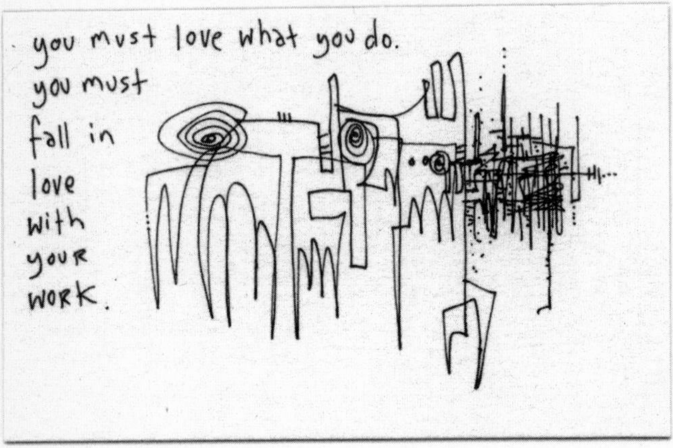
you must love what you do.
you must
fall in
love
with
your
work.

I need
love.
then i
need
straw-
berries.

hill

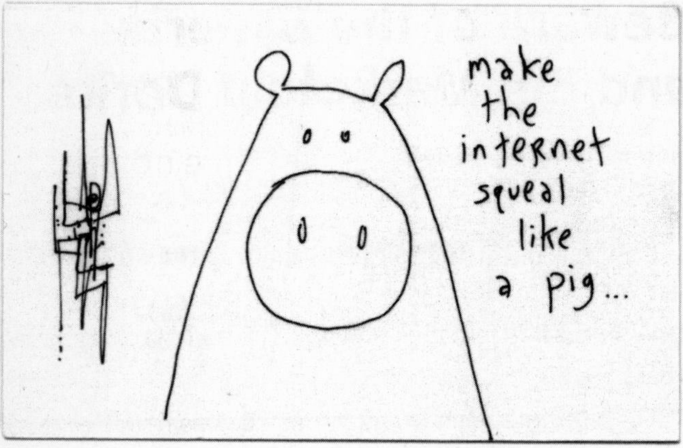
make
the
internet
squeal
like
a pig...

Beware of the Experts and the Marketing Dorks

THE EXPERTS AND THE MARKETING DORKS TELL us a lot of stuff.

Stuff designed to make them sound clever and make us part with our money.

Which is fine, but their shtick isn't the whole story. Buzzwords are not the word of God.

The Internet doesn't work the way it does because some clever person in New York or Shanghai has decided she needs your money.

No, it's something far more universal and egalitarian.

The Internet works best when we're all trying to share stuff. Not just the corporations and the Internet millionaires, but you, me, everybody else on this planet.

Sharing not just silly videos and photos of our cats, but stuff that matters. Big stuff and small stuff—where to find a decent Lebanese restaurant or a highly complex technical procedure.

Shared learning.

If we know anything worth knowing, chances are we'll find a way to get it online. And other people will do the same with their stuff—a great tree of shared knowledge, with everybody contributing their own unique "fruit" to the various branches, whatever they might be.

That's the most powerful thing about the Internet: it allows us to share knowledge, allows us to share learning—one of the most important forms of human interaction—faster and cheaper and easier than anything else that came before.

And shared learning can't be pushed through the pipes; it can only be pulled.

People will only pull knowledge off the tree if they want to, if they think there's something in it for them. And they, not you, get to decide what that "something" is.

As Sonia Simone of Copyblogger.com said, "If your business model is 'I want to make money on the Internet,' you're not going to get very far. The Internet is profoundly indifferent to your desire to make money with it."

The most important word on the Internet isn't "Search"; the most important Internet word is "Share."

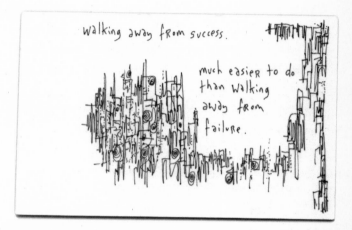

walking away from success.

much easier to do
than walking
away from
failure.

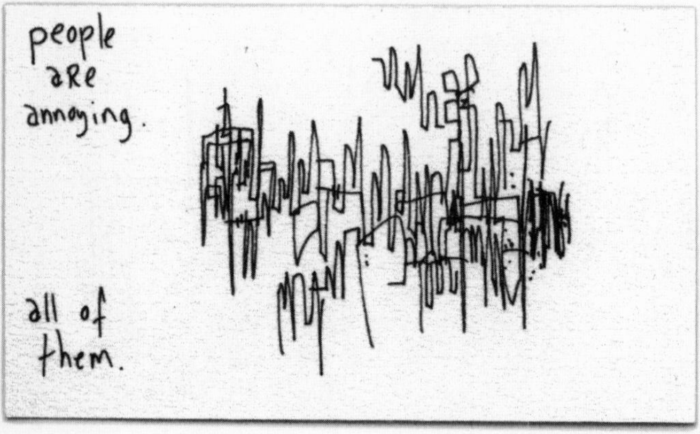
people
are
annoying.
all of
them.

hmmmm... that
kinda warrants a
"who the fuck
are you" response.

all art
is
longing.

The Best Thing About the Internet Is the People You Meet

MOST OF THE PEOPLE I CONSIDER FRIENDS these days I met through blogging. People like Seth Godin or Loic Le Meur or Doc Searls or Adriana Cronin-Lukas or Mark Earls or Kathy Sierra or David Brain.

We stumbled on each other's work online one day.

And somehow we started talking, leaving comments, trading e-mails.

And somehow things started to happen.

And this process never stops. It just keeps on happening, again and again.

These connections mean far more, are far more valuable, than a huge list of semianonymous readers.

The "readers" are nice, the "readers" have their place, but that's not where the real action is.

Worry about meaningful connections. The "audience" will take care of itself.

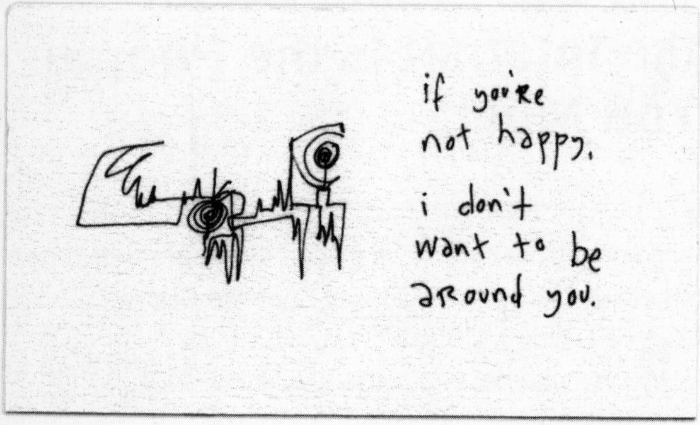
if you're
not happy,
i don't
want to be
around you.

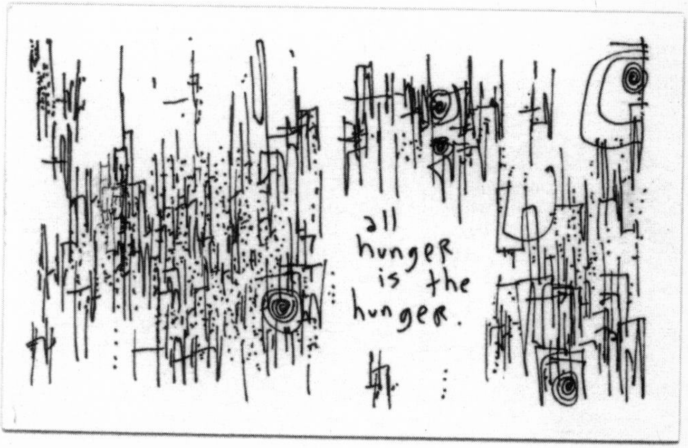
all
hunger
is the
hunger.

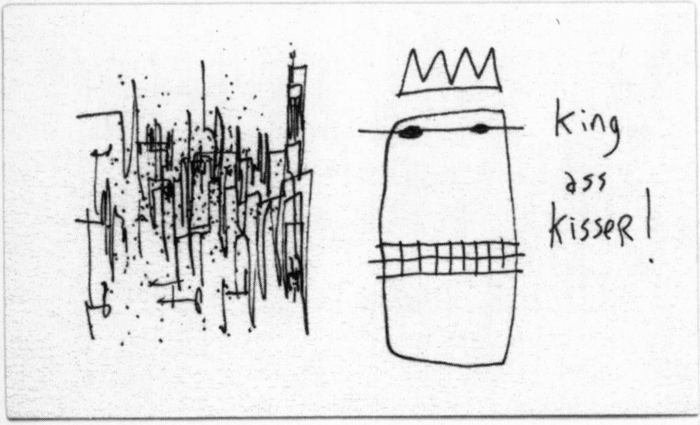
king ass kisser!

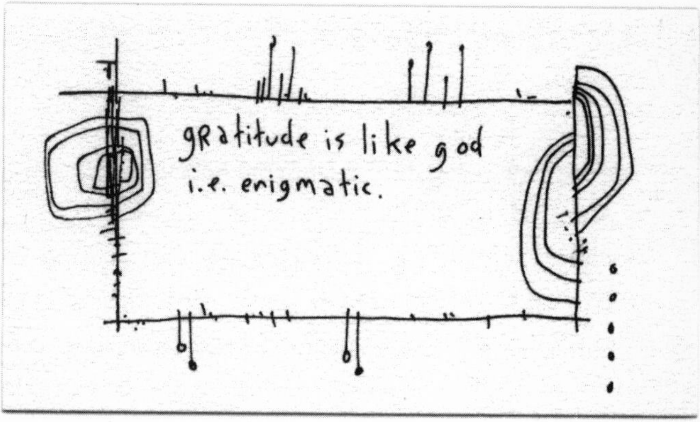
gratitude is like god
i.e. enigmatic.

Four Beacons

ARE YOU A BEACON?

A beacon is a navigation signal that tells you where you are when you're lost at sea.

We spend a lot of our careers being lost at sea . . . paddling away, not quite sure where we are, hoping to God that a big wave won't come along and swamp our little boat.

And we look for beacons to guide us, to give us hope, to tell us where we are, to show us where the standard is, to show us the way forward. Beacons can be people, products, businesses, or even ideas.

"Life might suck right now, but one day I'll land a kick-ass job as creative director for Crispin Porter!"

"Life might suck right now, but one day I'll write as good a novel as Jonathan Franzen!"

"Life might suck right now, but one day our product will be better than SAP or Oracle!"

These are beacons. . . .

Obviously, if you or your product is a beacon to other

people in your own industry, you have a considerable advantage going for you. Not to mention a really good reason to get up in the morning.

SO IN MY TYPICAL WAY, I'LL ASK YOU, ARE YOU A BEACON? IF NOT, DON'T YOU THINK YOU SHOULD BE?

With that in mind, here are four blogging beacons of mine—people who have inspired me over the years, people who allowed blogging to change their world, and the worlds around them, for the better. They're not my only beacons, of course, but they're certainly worth checking out; they've got plenty that one can learn from.

Fred Wilson (www.avc.com) was a successful venture capitalist who started blogging around seven or eight years ago. Besides being a good writer, his plain-speaking, affable manner got him a lot of fans, including people who were in need of venture capital. And it meant regular readers like me had someone to turn to for insight into that business; he opened a lot of eyes, made a rather mysterious world seem a lot more down-to-earth.

This meant that when the good deals were happening (i.e., when Twitter was on the hunt for funding), Fred could get in on the ground floor. Which, of course, helped his business to no end.

John T. Unger (www.johntunger.com) is an artist living in

rural Michigan. He makes iron firebowl sculptures, which he sells for big money. He first got the word out on his firebowls by blogging avidly, and by leaving comments on other blogs that he admired. Eventually he got sick of blogging, so he switched over to Twitter to do his main communication with the outside world. But by that time, business was already through the roof, so he could afford to. Blogging allowed him to find a way to sell art on his terms to people who actually cared about him, something I believe that a lot of artists could learn from.

Austin Kleon (www.austinkleon.com) is a young artist and writer who had a bit of initial success posting his cartoons and "Newspaper Blackout" poems on his blog. But then he hit it big-time when he posted his manifesto, "How to Steal Like an Artist," on his blog, which ended up getting downloaded many hundreds of thousands of times and landed him a massive book deal. "How to Steal" was a smart, passionate masterpiece of good advice to young people about how to succeed as an artist. It was pretty much the best thing I read in 2001.

Megan McArdle (www.theatlantic.com/megan-mcardle) is a libertarian economics wonk whose blog, JaneGalt.net, was so good, the *Economist* (the famous British newsweekly) offered her a job. She now writes as a senior editor for the *Atlantic* magazine. When she started JaneGalt she was a young, poor MBA graduate who decided her true passion was writing about economics. By taking the bold move of renouncing the typical MBA career in the bowels of corporations and simultaneously putting her work "out there" into the blogosphere, she became one of most respected political journalists in the country.

Yes, you can learn plenty from these names I just gave you, but there are thousands of other examples out there in the blogosphere, all easy enough to find if you start looking. Frankly, it isn't rocket science. By owning your own media (in this case, blogging), you own your own platform. Own your own platform, and you own your own career. Own your own career, and you own your own life. Own your own life, and that, my friends, is what freedom is all about.

relaxin'

miles davis

all careers end in failure eventually..........

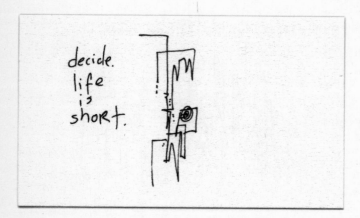

decide.
life
is
short.

your last
day on
Earth
will be
the
greatest
gift you
ever received.

Now Quit Your Yappin'

GO MAKE STUFF

Telling people how great the Internet is is easy. Everybody knows that already. The hard part is knowing that the ball is in your court, knowing that now you have this AMAZING tool, knowing that there are no more excuses. So now you have to go and make stuff. The Internet can't do that for you; the Internet can only remove certain obstacles. And it already did that. A long time ago.

The Internet has made it so that we have no choice but to be creative.

So in the last few paragraphs of this very short read (jump ahead to page 115), I'm saving my best for last.

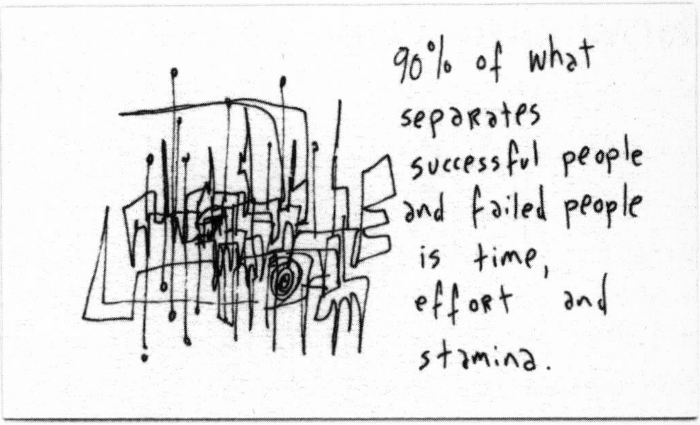
90% of what
separates
successful people
and failed people
is time,
effort and
stamina.

are you alive?
prove it.

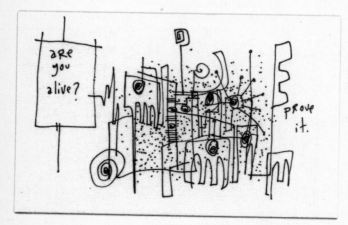

internal
monologue

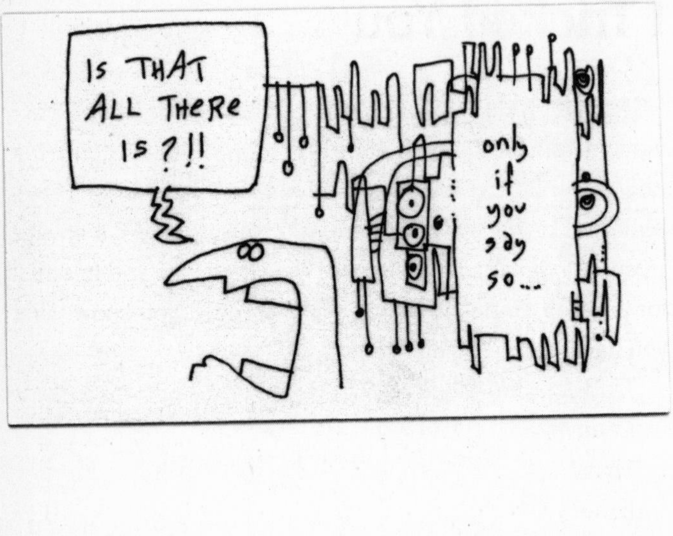
IS THAT ALL THERE IS?!!
only if you say so...

I Tricked You

I SPENT THE LAST FEW THOUSAND WORDS TELL-
ing you about the power of the Internet, when all along, the
power wasn't there. The power is somewhere else. That's
right, the power is within you—the same place it's always
been. All the advent of Internet did was allow you to see it
for yourself. And now that you have seen it, you know what
you have to do. You must act. Today.

Find your Freedom.

Create.

Right now.

Exactly.

Good luck. And thanks for reading, seriously. Godspeed.

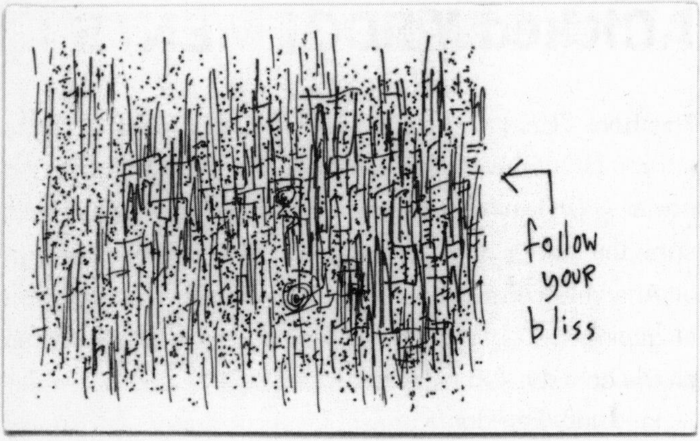
follow
your
bliss

ACKNOWLEDGEMENTS

This book would not have been possible if it weren't for the people around me, the ever-growing gapingvoid extended family, all working their tails off to keep the show on the road, all constantly making sure my game is constantly raised.

Ana, my girlfriend. Jason, my business partner and CEO of gapingvoid LLC. Laura, our head of operations. David on the computer. Their families, especially Catherine, Paul, Luca, Alex, and Mrs. Korman. Lisa, my agent. Adrian, my publisher at Portfolio. Jillian, my editor. Julia, her rock-star assistant. Seth Godin, who first introduced me to Adrian.

Second, to the many customers and clients who have supported the work over the years—especially Rackspace Hosting, Dewar's Whisky, and Babson College.

Last, to my friend and fellow blogging cartoonist, Austin Kleon (www.austinkleon.com), whose genius masterpiece *Steal Like An Artist* inspired me to get writing again ASAP . . .